Clark Fork River

Greg Thomas

Frank Amato
PORTLAND

Volume 5, Number 2, 1997

About the Author

Greg Thomas writes for various newspapers and magazines, including regular columns for the New York *Times* and the *Missoulian. River Journal: Clark Fork* is his second book. He is currently working on a collection of fly-fishing essays. After stints in Seattle, Washington, Jackson, Wyoming, Sun Valley, Idaho and Missoula, Hamilton and Gallatin Gateway, Montana, Thomas has returned to Missoula and the Clark Fork River where he lives with his Labradors, Shadow and Moose.

◆

Acknowledgments

Many thanks to my father, Fred, mother, Rita, and sister, Kim, for all their support. Also, to Shadow and Moose, my two best fishing buddies—they never complain about sloppy casts or the fact that I never leave them a cold beer. And many thanks to all my fishing pals in Missoula (Jim Nave, Dan Sumerfield, Kent Sullivan, Greg Henry, Jeff Herman, Torrey and Skip Cenis and Scott Brown, among others) who keep even the slowest days more than a little interesting. Many thanks to Jim Toth of the Grizzle Hackle Fly Shop for providing the flies for the fly plates. Finally, thanks to Frank Amato for allowing me to write *River Journal: Clark Fork*.

◆

Series Editor: Frank Amato—Kim Koch

Subscriptions:
Softbound: $35.00 for one year (four issues) $65.00 for two years
Hardbound Limited Editions: $95.00 one year, $170.00 for two years

Design: Kathy Johnson Photography: Greg Thomas (unless otherwise noted)
Fly plates photographed by: Jim Schollmeyer
Map: Kathy Johnson
Softbound ISBN: 1-57188-091-7, Hardbound ISBN: 1-57188-092-5
(Hardbound Edition Limited to 350-500 Copies)

Clark Fork River
M O N T A N A

The Clark Fork changes from a placid, flat-surfaced river to a brawling, rapid-laden torrent at Rest Stop Rapids near Alberton. This photo offers a glimpse at the last calm water before entering Rest Stop Rapids and, just downstream, the Alberton Gorge.

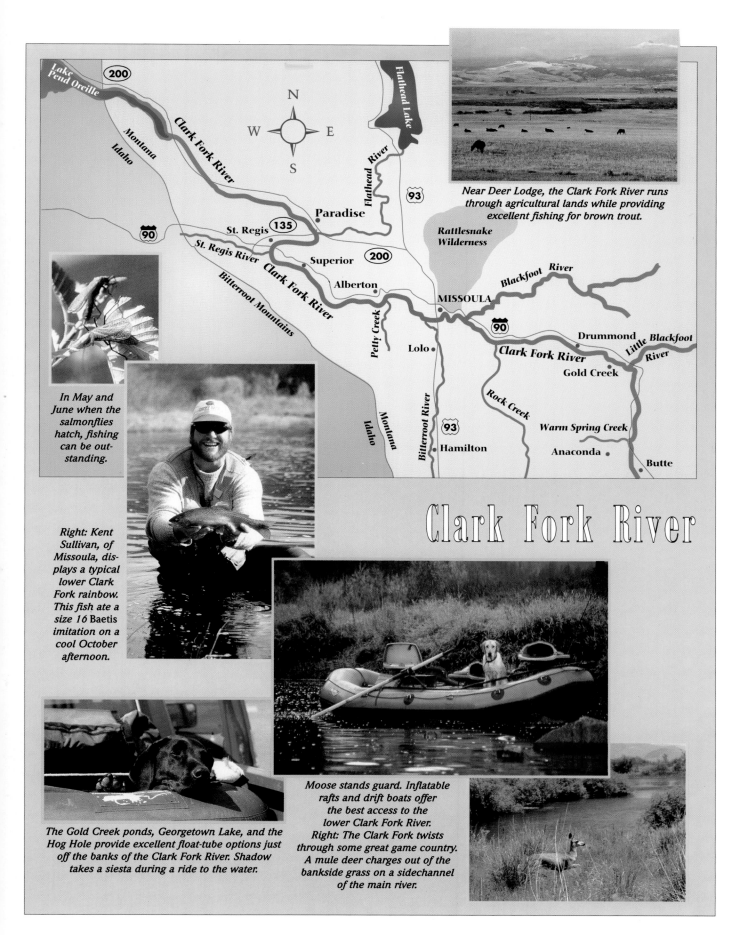

Clark Fork River

Near Deer Lodge, the Clark Fork River runs through agricultural lands while providing excellent fishing for brown trout.

In May and June when the salmonflies hatch, fishing can be outstanding.

Right: Kent Sullivan, of Missoula, displays a typical lower Clark Fork rainbow. This fish ate a size 16 Baetis imitation on a cool October afternoon.

The Gold Creek ponds, Georgetown Lake, and the Hog Hole provide excellent float-tube options just off the banks of the Clark Fork River. Shadow takes a siesta during a ride to the water.

Moose stands guard. Inflatable rafts and drift boats offer the best access to the lower Clark Fork River.
Right: The Clark Fork twists through some great game country. A mule deer charges out of the bankside grass on a sidechannel of the main river.

If anglers want quality fishing to continue on the Clark Fork, they must join hands with environmental organizations, like The Clark Fork Coalition and American Rivers, to protect the resource. This prime rainbow wants your support.

Clark Fork River

Introduction

If you are looking for a good example of poor resource management in the West, look no farther than the banks of western Montana's largest river—the Clark Fork.

In its infancy, birthed two million years ago by glacial scouring and the flow of two small streams, it was as pure as a waterway could be. Today, especially when the water runs toxic red and fish kills occur, like they did in 1989, the Clark Fork reflects its most recent history—100 years of mineral extraction at its headwaters, massive timber cut from its banks and irrigation water sucked straight from its palsied heart. Unfortunately, the Clark Fork's single greatest contribution to fly fishing may very well be the example it displays. Take a look at the Clark Fork's problems and the message is clear: hard rock mining and shoddy timber harvests are the single most direct threat to Montana's sport fisheries.

Still, the Clark Fork, which begins at the confluence of Warm Spring and Silver Bow creeks near Butte and ends nearly 300 miles west at Idaho's Lake Pend Oreille, provides the avid fly fisher excellent opportunities for big rainbow, cutthroat and brown trout, which is a testament to the determination of our quarry and the resiliency a river can display. The Clark Fork is no sissy.

Despite its opportunities, the Clark Fork receives little ink from the outdoors writers and little merit from fly fishers who compare it to those noted Big Sky Country neighbors, like the Bighorn, Yellowstone, Missouri, Beaverhead and Big Hole. Likely, the Clark Fork's tainted past, those existing scars on its banks, like piles of mine tailings between Butte and Anaconda, and a sketchy future steer anglers away.

That neglect is unfortunate for those who refuse to sample its goods, so to speak. But, that cold-shoulder is a blessing for those who appreciate the Clark Fork's easy access, excellent scenery, varied currents, uncrowded conditions and large trout. Oh, it's true, you can bump into a few rafts during the summer float season, especially on the lower river between Missoula and St. Regis, but pressure on the Clark Fork is definitely not like that on the Big Hole during the salmonfly hatch, for instance.

While the Clark Fork may look weathered in some sections,

most noted near Butte, Anaconda and Warm Springs, other areas are extremely gorgeous, nearly pristine, and they can be very productive in a fly fishing and scenic sense.

Most people refer to the Clark Fork in two sections: the upper and lower reaches. The upper stretch takes in about 125 miles of water from Warm Springs to Milltown Dam. The lower river extends from Milltown, just a few miles east of Missoula, downstream for nearly 200 miles to Lake Pend Oreille in Idaho. Below Paradise and the mouth of the Flathead River, the Clark Fork ceases as a quality trout stream. Big smallmouth bass and some scary northern pike are available in this section.

At its headwaters, the Clark Fork flows through the vast Deer Lodge Valley. To the southwest, the rugged, jagged, often snowcapped Pintler and Deer Lodge mountains reign. To the east, rolling, timbered foothills race away from the river. The valley bottom itself is willow-lined where it is not divided into massive green fields of alfalfa. Whitetail deer, a few elk, mule deer and various birds call the valley home.

The river rates about 10 to 15 yards wide near the head-waters and it twists and turns religiously. It is classic brown trout water with brushy banks, deep undercuts and dark holes. To float the river in a boat or raft is overdoing it. The upper section is best waded by fly fishers.

Near Clinton, just downstream from the mouth of Rock Creek, the river winds through narrow canyons with densely timbered slopes, when it is not slicing through the modest valley bottom. Cottonwoods and willows follow the banks. Mule deer and elk frequent the steep, rocky slopes above the river. Whitetails claim the valley bottom.

The river rates about 20 to 30 yards wide in most places, although it can narrow to almost nothing in places. Braids and side channels abound. A drift boat or raft allows anglers to cover lots of water during spring and early summer when flows are up, but by late summer and during fall, the river is best waded.

The mix of fish between the mouth of Rock Creek and Milltown Reservoir, which lies about 16 miles downstream from Clinton, is about equal: 50 percent rainbow/50 percent browns.

A small to medium size stream above Milltown Dam, the

The upper Clark Fork is classic brown trout water. Hit the banks with a hopper, probe the riffles with a caddis nymph, or strip a wicked streamer through the deepest holes—a fish measuring between 12 and 20 inches will likely eat your offering.

Clark Fork changes its face by broadening out considerably, just as it enters the Missoula Valley. From there, it banks up against the Bitterroot Mountains to the south and follows their line downstream to the west. The river provides massive riffles, mile-long, flat-surfaced glides, and questionably deep holes. It boils around massive rock outcroppings, winds through open hayfields, braids occasionally, curls under 30-foot-tall dirt banks, and penetrates violently through narrow fissures.

All of the lower river can be intimidating water, but there is one stretch that takes the cake. Just downstream from Petty Creek, the river raises its hackles as it cuts through Alberton Gorge and Cyr Canyon. Floaters who offer themselves to the water will encounter 20 miles of Class IV waves. Rapid names such as Tumbleweed, Boateater and Fang scare off most fly fishers. However, some of the river's biggest rainbow trout and most prolific populations persist in that stretch.

As the Clark Fork exits Cyr Canyon, it again flattens out, settles down and continues, forever it seems, west. The river will carry that size and description to the Idaho state line and its finality at Lake Pend Oreille.

Even without the Clark Fork's varied, wonderful scenery, a river that is capable of kicking out 20 to 30 rainbow or brown trout during its best days, strong fish that may stretch 25 inches or more, is worthy of a fly caster's attention. It has definitely caught mine.

For me, the Clark Fork holds special appeal. It is the river where I cut my fly fishing teeth. You may have seen me behind the Red Lion Hotel near downtown Missoula a few years back. I was the fool standing waist-deep in the river during early spring with a pair of shorts on. I couldn't afford neoprene waders; attending the University of Montana took every spare cent I could find.

I spent a lot of time in the river during my college years and I nearly froze to death more than once. But, the river provided a sanctuary from the frustration of college life, especially for a particular student who put academic education on the back burner. Plus, it was pretty cool to land a big rainbow or bull trout at the mouth of Rattlesnake Creek with a live audience shouting encouragement from hotel and restaurant windows behind me.

Sitting on the tailgate of my truck on a classic, calm Big Sky Country summer morning, the sun already heating my skin at 8 a.m. and big, puffy, white cumulous clouds building to the west, the likely question when considering the Clark Fork River is: "Where do I start?" Your answer, of course, is "What's hatching?"

Probably the most effective way to fish the river is by chasing hatches—and there are a number of good ones.

The upper river receives healthy doses of *Baetis* and caddis early in the year. After runoff, the caddis hatch is immense and fishing can be awesome. Fly fishers should also watch for the big salmonflies below the mouth of Rock Creek in mid- to late June. Later, in July and August, pale morning duns can be found on the water and pods of trout will pluck them under the surface. Trico mayflies may appear, forcing fly fishers to work size 20 or smaller dry flies off of minuscule 6X or 7X tippet.

Then, in August and September, the upper river's brown trout turn their daytime attention—and I mean all of it—to grasshoppers. Throw a Dave's Hopper along an undercut bank; cast it next to a grassy, hay bank; drift it over a deep hole; drown it and swing it through a shallow riffle; a brown trout will find it and quickly eat it. Darrel Gadbow, a writer for the *Missoulian*, and an avid Clark Fork fly fisher, nailed a 28-inch brown on the upper river on a hopper pattern in August 1996.

Big browns live in the upper Clark Fork, but they are difficult to land on such small water—it rates 10 to 15 yards wide in most places with lots of downed snags, undercut banks and various debris offering those big trout plenty of options when attempting to part your leader.

Hoppers offer the only consistent surface action for the big boys. During other seasons, anglers must drag the big, ugly stuff, like Woolly Buggers and sculpins, through brush jams and the deep holes to draw strikes.

The lower river enjoys its fair share of excellent hatches, too. *Baetis* mayflies, also called blue-wing olives, may provide the most productive fishing of the year. Watch for their presence throughout the lower section in late April and May, and again in late September through mid-November.

Often coinciding with the *Baetis* is an early hatch of caddis along with the emergence of *Skwala* stoneflies. The stoneflies will taper off sometime in May, but caddis persist through summer. In July, after runoff, pale morning duns, green drakes and grasshoppers take over. As fall nears, Tricos litter the river's surface each morning and pods of big rainbows slurp them down in the backeddies and foam lines. In September, mahogany duns kick in as the Tricos taper off. Then, the *Baetis* extravaganza returns.

Following is a list of the Clark Fork's sections, ranging from the brown trout water of the upper river to the big, roily currents and the rainbow trout of the lower river. Thrown in on the side are diversions to the Clark Fork's wonderful tributary streams. Also noted are the river's personalities and history.

Take a seat in the bow, I'll take the oars. Hang on tight as we rip through the gorge. And always, no matter where we are on this river, from the abused headwaters to the pristine canyons, take in all that this river has to say; the Clark Fork is trying to send a clear, enduring message. Take it with you to your home water and please leave something with the Clark Fork. The future of all our fisheries depends on each of us understanding this message.

Hard-rock Mining: The Clark Fork's ugly past and its sketchy future

It would be nice to sit back in an easy chair and daydream strictly about that beautiful pine-tree-laced place on the map called western Montana. You know, dredge up some images of big rainbow and brown trout on the end of your line while floating down the Clark Fork River in a drift boat. But, that would be a crime.

Unfortunately, anyone who's interested in the Clark Fork or, for that matter, any other river in the state, must address those issues that taint its past, effect it presently and threaten to devastate its fisheries in the future.

The Clark Fork, simply put, is a mess. Not that it hasn't come a long way in recent years with the help of environmental groups like the Clark Fork-Pend Oreille Coalition. But, the potential for massive fish kills exists as heavily on the Clark Fork today as on any other river in the West, if not the world. And, water quality stands to get worse if more major mine proposals get approval on its tributaries.

At its headwaters the Clark Fork River country is a land of famous records. "World's largest open pit mine", a mile-wide, 1,000-foot-deep wound that recently filled with 20 million

A large river by the time it reaches Petty Creek, the lower Clark Fork offers excellent dry-fly opportunities on its flat surface.

Mike Nave and Mandy examine a typical Clark Fork brown trout.

gallons of musty, toxic water at Butte, and the "world's largest smokestack", a 585-foot-tall smelter with a 60-foot-wide mouth, at Anaconda. "The Stack", which contains almost 7 million bricks, and towers over miles of mine tailings, stands as a testament to the Clark Fork's darkest days.

Due to those records, the Clark Fork's headwaters, including Silver Bow and Warm Springs creeks, hold the unenviable title of nation's largest Superfund clean-up site. Yes, it is true—environmental devastation right here in picturesque Montana; do not kid yourself—environmental disasters are happening all over this state, this place called Montana that harbors arguably the best collection of trout waters in the world.

◆

Not as well known as the salmonfly, smaller stoneflies, like this Skwala, *tempt trout to the surface during spring.*

Materials extracted from the Berkeley Pit in Butte during the corrupt copper king period in the late 1800s and those tailings deposited at Anaconda after being broken down in the smelter, remain an ugly scar on the banks of the upper river. You can see the black piles of rubble extending beside Interstate 90 for 25 miles between Anaconda and Butte. If you have only seen Montana through the glossy travel brochures and picturesque television advertisements, those mine tailing piles will open your eyes. And, it's those tailings that have a direct effect on the Clark Fork's trout populations.

Mining in the Butte area, formerly referred to as the "richest hill on earth" (now an unsightly hole in the ground), began in 1864 when placer miners arrived. By 1874, silver claims were made in the area and throngs of miners, and capital investors arrived. The money, opportunity, politics and, of course, corruption was raging full-steam ahead (the corruption still does today!).

A single copper vein alone produced 50 million pounds in 1887. At that time, over 20,000 people lived in Butte, amidst an atmosphere of wild brawling, drinking, eating and hard work. The mines ran full-tilt, day and night. The restaurants, bars, cafes, opium dens and cathouses followed suit. It is reported that in the 1890s, toxic fumes darkened the air enough that streetlights remained on during the day. Health problems, like cancer and respiratory diseases, took a toll. Environmental catastrophe was an afterthought.

In the 1930s, the price of copper fell and Butte began its era of demise. In 1983, the Anaconda Company closed the Berkeley Pit. Butte turned its back on a century of environmental sabotage and turned its eyes toward a sketchy future. Unfortunately, the Clark Fork's trout do not have that option. Neither does the area's wildlife.

In 1996, nearly 350 snow geese landed on the water in the pit and died overnight. Surprise, surprise. Of course, officials for Atlantic Richfield Co. (ARCO) said the pit was likely not to blame for the birds' deaths. When the pit overflows into Butte, as many fear it will, and people die in droves, ARCO will probably still try to maintain their innocence.

Unfortunately, the truth is, many of Montana's residents allow themselves to be brainwashed by multi-million dollar ad campaigns that shoot down clean water initiatives, like I-122, which failed at the polls in 1996. Grassroots groups that try to preserve what is left of Montana's clean water ultimately find themselves up against the monetary wall. In a time of mass media, those who can buy ad space on television and get their message across, whether it is true or not, will likely win most battles.

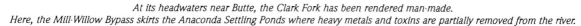

As recently as 1989, the upper Clark Fork endured flash floods that resulted in heavy metal contamination and major fish kills. That contamination sent about 5,000 fish belly-up, including more than 2,000 brown trout. And some of those were very sizable specimens. The potential for major fish kills are as high today as they were on July 12, 1989.

According to Meg Nelson, executive director for the Clark Fork-Pend Oreille Coalition based in Missoula, similar fish kills should be expected unless the mine tailings are removed from the area.

"In terms of fishing, we need to clean up those waters, once and for all," Nelson said. "If we don't, we'll always see floods of heavy metals coming into the streams."

Finding a place to put the material is the problem. There are literally endless piles of it at Anaconda, where silver and copper was brought to be rendered by the smelter. Butte couldn't do it as the area harbors very little water. But, Anaconda held an attraction—Silver Bow and Warm Spring creeks. Unfortunately, those two creeks suffer the effects of Butte's mining history and they aren't about to shed their past anytime soon; most people agree, the upper Clark Fork will fully recover when the next ice age arrives.

According to "Defender of the Clark Fork", Wayne Hadley, who happens to be a Clark Fork biologist for Montana Department of Fish, Wildlife and Parks, fish kills probably occur in the river much more frequently than most of us believe.

"I have always thought that we have numerous fish kills in January and February due to bank sluffage that brings heavy metals into the stream," Hadley said. "I'm sure there are lots of fish kills that we are not aware of. You can see fish dying one day and go back two days later and there are no signs of them. I think the raccoons and birds pick them up pretty quick. I would guess that we don't know about one fish kill in 10."

Toxic contamination isn't the upper river's only problem. Nutrient overload from waste water treatment plants and dewatering by irrigators effectively rob the river of oxygen, turning the water into a moss-bed in some sections by midsummer. When you cast a fly at that time, you will strip sticky, gooey moss from the hook after every cast. Productive fishing is rendered futile.

Problems affecting fish and the residents who live along

◆

At its headwaters near Butte, the Clark Fork has been rendered man-made.
Here, the Mill-Willow Bypass skirts the Anaconda Settling Ponds where heavy metals and toxins are partially removed from the river.

the banks of the Clark Fork are not restricted to the upper river. Downstream at Milltown Dam near Missoula, six million cubic yards of contaminated sediment, which worked its way down from Butte and Anaconda, rest, like a loaded gun with the hammer cocked, behind that aging structure. Arsenic levels in that contamination are high, effecting the drinking water of Bonner and Milltown. Concern over the structural soundness of Milltown Dam, which was built in the early 1900s and has an existing crack in it, is growing.

Within the confines of the nation's largest Superfund cleanup site, the Clark Fork offers some huge trout. Greg Henry, of Missoula, puts the hurt on a monster rainbow in a spillway between ponds as Moose and Shadow look on.

"Depending on who you talk to there's a lot of concern about the dam," Nelson said. "The dam doesn't contribute very much power for Missoula and if it were to burst it would flood the city. And all of that contaminated sediment would flow downstream."

Some of it did in 1996. In fact, in early February that year Montana Power Company opened the gates on Milltown Dam due to fears that a massive ice jam, racing down the Blackfoot River, might wipe out the dam. The idea was to drop the water level behind Milltown Dam so that the eight-mile ice jam would grind to a halt.

Opening the gates sent massive amounts of cadmium, arsenic, copper and zinc downstream. Copper levels alone measured 400 parts per billion below the dam. Upstream at Deer Lodge, where ice jams scoured the river bottom and banks, copper levels hit 960 parts per billion. At the same time, copper levels tested 64 parts per billion at the headwaters of the Clark Fork in Silver Bow Creek, which has been labeled an industrial ditch. The state limit for copper is 18 parts per billion. Many of the Clark Fork's rainbows died, especially those in the stretch of river that runs through the heart of Missoula. So much for an excellent after-work trout fishery.

While the Clark Fork's past contributes heavily to its present health, it is the future that most frightens Nelson and her organization. The Clark Fork's future, in fact the future of many great Montana streams, should frighten every serious fly fisher, too.

Proposals for more massive mines on the Clark Fork's tributaries, the Blackfoot River northeast of Missoula, Rock Creek west of Missoula, and Rock Creek near Knoxon, seriously threaten the continued health of the river.

"There's been a resurgence of interest in hard-rock mining

and that's a tremendous threat to the Clark Fork," Nelson said. "People just don't learn from past mistakes. These mines could devastate the tributaries located along the Clark Fork and, ultimately, the main river itself."

Heap leach mining is a method that big corporations, Canadian in many cases, use to extricate small amounts of gold from mounds of bulldozed land. That land is unearthed and cyanide is blasted against it, the ground being turned to rubble, dotted with chunks of gold.

"The mine proposed on the Blackfoot would be about 70 percent the size of the Berkeley Pit in Butte. It would be one of the largest cyanide heap leach mines in the world.

"The mine on Rock Creek near Knoxon would be a silver and copper mine, located just 25 miles from Lake Pend Oreille," Nelson added. "It too would be one of the world's largest mines and it would be very damaging to the Clark Fork."

That mine on Rock Creek would remove an estimated 10,000 tons of copper- and silver-bearing ore a day. Production could last 30 years, leaving the clean-up and aftereffects as the responsibility of the next generation, i.e. your children.

On Rock Creek west of Missoula, one of the best trout fisheries and one of the most scenic areas in the state, Cable Mountain Mining is proposing a cyanide heap-leach operation in Cornish Gulch, just downstream from Gilles Bridge. American Gem Mountain is planning a sapphire project in the West Fork area, in the Rock Creek headwaters. Both of those proposed mines could ruin Rock Creek and they would contribute to further demise on the Clark Fork.

If trout fishing is to remain an option in the West, in the world for that matter, past blunders, like those in Butte and Anaconda, and the currently proposed maladies must stop. Unfortunately, most people endear their wallets rather than the state's trout streams. Montana's public officials continue to lessen water quality standards—their retirement, courtesy of the mining companies, currently looks quite rosy.

Are we going to take this? Shouldn't we stop bickering over the status of a dry-fly fisher versus a nymph fisher and organize our thoughts and efforts toward preserving our fisheries for ourselves and future generations? In my mind, trout are everything. If we are not going to protect them, why bother with anything? We might as well be compost.

Every angler, whether a fly fisher, a spin fisher or even a bait-soaker, has a stake in the Clark Fork. Every one of us sees beauty in the river, enjoys being on it and we should try to save it. Get active and support efforts to quell mineral extraction from the river's banks and tributaries. The existence of trout, not only on the Clark Fork, but every water in Montana, depends on it.

The Upper Clark Fork from Warm Springs to Deer Lodge—precarious beginnings

At its headwaters, the Clark Fork River isn't really a river. Instead, it's a series of ponds, spillways, sloughs, toxic ditches and bypasses. However, it is also one of the best places in the state to hook a trophy rainbow or brown trout.

Trout exceeding three pounds are regularly landed in the first few miles of the river—several fish over 10 pounds will show up each year, too.

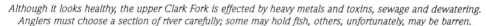

Although it looks healthy, the upper Clark Fork is effected by heavy metals and toxins, sewage and dewatering. Anglers must choose a section of river carefully; some may hold fish, others, unfortunately, may be barren.

With the Anaconda-Pintler Wilderness as a backdrop, the upper Clark Fork offers excellent caddis hatches almost every day during the summer. Gary LaFontaine conducted research for his definitive book, Caddisflies, *on the upper Clark Fork.*

◆

Most of the large fish are taken in the first 10 miles of the river where, strangely enough, the nation's largest Superfund cleanup site exists. There are several factors that contribute to the river's success.

First, a series of stillwaters, called the Anaconda Settling Pond System, developed to filter out mining wastes from Silver Bow Creek, rests just upstream from where the Clark Fork begins. Those ponds serve as a nurturing ground for rainbow and brown trout that are stocked by Montana Department of Fish, Wildlife and Parks. A few of the fish may be wild.

Wild or not, those trout grow quickly on a variety of aquatic insects—a literal smorgasbord. It is believed that the temperature of the ponds rises too high during summer so trout bail out over the spillways into the river. During winter, ice may cause the fish to do the same thing. For whatever reason, when that happens the trout are deposited directly into the Clark Fork.

I have taken browns up to 26 inches long in the Mill Willow Bypass and downstream between the Pond 3 Spillway and Warm Springs Bridge. Dan Summerfield of Missoula, took a rainbow one winter that easily weighed six pounds. It might have weighed 10. He didn't weigh it. Instead, he returned it to the river, just as the regulations for all of the Anaconda Settling Pond System, the Mill-Willow Bypass and the Clark Fork itself, downstream to Warm Springs Bridge, require. It's catch-and-release, artificial flies and lures only.

While big trout provide a tremendous rush when hooked

in such a small stream, it is the upper river's resident trout, populations of browns that sometimes reach 2,000 fish a mile (on a stream that rates about one-fourth the size of the Madison!), that are its trademark. Those trout and caddisflies, that is.

According to Hadley at Montana Department of Fish, Wildlife and Parks, brown trout on the upper Clark Fork average between 12 and 14 inches. And their population, although it too fights the effects of heavy metals and frequent fish kills, is strong.

"A nice fish in that section goes about 16 inches," Hadley said, "and a real exceptional trout would go 20 inches or more. There are very few fish over 20 inches, just a few rainbows and browns that slip down from the ponds."

The very upper reaches of the river can be broken into three sections: from the Pond 3 Spillway to Warm Springs Bridge; from Warm Springs Bridge to Galen Bridge and from Galen Bridge to Deer Lodge. All of these sections are classic caddisfly water—the banks are brush-riddled, the river bottom fertile, and the surface slow.

The section near Deer Lodge, for that matter all of the upper river, is where angling author and publisher Gary LaFontaine, a.k.a. Mr. Caddis, studied the insects for his definitive book, Caddisflies. According to LaFontaine, the early caddis hatch on the upper Clark Fork is well worth hitting. To miss it is a sin.

"It's the thickest hatch you can imagine," he said. "I think everyone should see it once in their life. If you were standing 60 feet upstream from me, you'd have a hard time seeing me through the flies. They are an absolute blizzard in the evening and the fish just go wild."

The upper Clark hosts two caddis species and they are both netmakers. The spotted sedge (Hydropsyche) is about a size 12 mottled-wing insect with a brown or dull yellow body, almost a rust color.

The other type is the Little Sister sedge (Cheumatopsyche), which is closely related to the spotted sedge, but is slightly smaller. It runs about a size 16 with a tan wing and body. Fortunately, these caddis are the predominant species across Montana—if you learn to fish them on the Clark Fork you pretty much have the entire state nailed for caddis fishing.

"They emerge as soon as runoff is over, which usually occurs on the upper Clark Fork in late June or early July," LaFontaine said. "People see those fish rolling and taking insects in the surface film so they tie on a dry-fly and that is a mistake. The fish are taking pupae in the surface film that are half-in, half-out of the water. When the pupa emerges, it's the fully-formed insect with a sheath around it. The sheath is clear and transparent and it holds tiny air bubbles.

"The fly that they will take is the Emergent Sparkle Pupa," LaFontaine added. "The reason it's special is it's tied with Antron yarn and that Antron mimics those air bubbles."

LaFontaine suggests fishing this pattern with floatant on the wing so it rides half-in, half-out of the water like the natural. It should be fished dead-drift with little movement.

If fly fishers can't take trout on the Emergent Pupa, try a Diving Caddis.

"It's a wet fly that I like to fish unweighted," LaFontaine said. "I cast upstream and let it dead drift just under the surface. I use an Elk Hair Caddis or an X-caddis as the dry-fly indicator and I'll drop the diving caddis about nine inches below the dry-fly."

Upper Clark Fork fly fishers may also encounter egg-laying female caddis. Generally, they can be seen in the air before fish start rising to them. Then, during the last hour of light, the females return to the river to deposit their eggs. That is when the fish key on them.

In that situation, LaFontaine fishes a Diving Caddis in various colors. Choose the pattern that matches the color of the naturals.

Look for most of the caddis action to occur in the evening, just before dark. However, fly fishers can nail trout all day long, in fact all year long (during the winter season, too) if they fish a free-living caddis larva.

"I like to fish those in size 12, 14 and 16 and I like bright green patterns best," LaFontaine said. "It's a really good searching pattern that can work all day."

While caddisflies provide the best action on the upper river, there are other important emergences.

Beginning in March and April, a few *Baetis* mayflies come off and the trout will turn to the top for them. They appear again in September, October and early November as the water cools after the hot summer months.

The tiny Trico mayfly also comes off in the fall, lasting from

---

The Hog Hole offers float-tubers an excellent shot at trophy brown and rainbow trout. Considered difficult to fish by most standards, patience plays a key role in an angler's success.

Even during the winter season, you can catch trout in the upper Clark Fork between Deer Lodge and the mouth of Rock Creek. However, during summer, the river suffers from chronic dewatering and moss and algae growth. Big browns can be had, but they are less populous than in the upper river.

late August through September. Brown trout will form pods and feed on those Tricos as they accumulate in the backeddies and slack-water pools.

The upper Clark Fork winds and cuts through the Deer Lodge Valley, creating lots of mud banks that are laced with willows. This is where cranefly larvae live. When the first high flows arrive, usually in April or May, these cranefly larvae are washed right out of banks and the trout gorge on them.

Grasshoppers are the most important terrestrial on the upper Clark Fork and they fly out of the hayfields en masse,

beginning in late July. Their presence will last into September.

You can literally tie a grasshopper to the end of your leader at 10 a.m. and leave it on until the sun begins fading. During the hopper season, those browns will hold under the cut banks, log jams and at the bottom of deep holes. However, if a hopper is smacked onto the surface and drifted within inches of the bank, they will come out to get it.

If you arrive at the upper Clark Fork and find no hatch of note, tie on a big Woolly Bugger or sculpin. Brown trout are brown trout wherever you find them.

Run those Buggers and sculpins through the deepest riffles, between the nastiest snags and along the tailouts of pools. There are too many trout in the upper river to think that every one of them could refuse a streamer. Oh yea, bring lots of extra flies, the upper Clark Fork is a fly eater if I've ever seen one.

First Interlude: The Hog Hole

When you first glance at the Anaconda Settling Pond System, it might resemble a war-torn landscape. A burm rises here, a pile of rocks sits there. The entire landscape shows signs of relocation. Vegetation grows in some places, in others the earth is bare.

This may be your first impression: I am as close to hell as I ever want to get. However, the ponds hold some appealing aspects, not the least being lunker rainbow and brown trout in the four- to 14-pound range! Plus, the ponds attract all variety of waterfowl and shorebirds. And, when the sun sets over the western mountains, the sky lighting up in crimson slashes, this color reflected onto a tranquil surface, you may even call the ponds beautiful. It helps if a huge trout is bending your rod like a green twig.

The first time I visited the ponds, there are six in all, I launched my float tube on the most famous one—the Hog Hole. I didn't catch a fish that evening, but I witnessed a rise like I

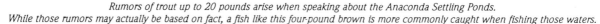

Rumors of trout up to 20 pounds arise when speaking about the Anaconda Settling Ponds. While those rumors may actually be based on fact, a fish like this four-pound brown is more commonly caught when fishing those waters.

The Gold Creek Ponds offer an interesting diversion when taking time away from the Clark Fork. Here, Sarah Hoskins, from Boulder, Colorado, releases a fish under the watchful eye of some old mining equipment.

had never seen. Just as the sun dropped, huge trout exited from the water in wild cartwheels, lengthy jumps and even sedate rises. The scene reminded me of southeast Alaska and a fresh batch of silver salmon moving into freshwater on the incoming tide. The size of the fish was comparable to silver salmon, too! I did not doubt why the pond received its name.

While the ponds were built to settle out mining wastes, surprisingly, aquatic vegetation grows readily. And where there is dense aquatic vegetation there exists heavy populations of aquatic insects. And where there are lots of aquatic insects (you're catching on aren't you) there are generally a lot of big trout. That is the case at the ponds.

It was not until the early 1980s that a small hit-group of fly fishers spearheaded an assault on the settling pond's population of large trout. Most fly fishers just didn't believe trout could live in that mess. Browns up to 14 pounds and rainbows over 10 pounds were taken before other anglers caught on to the secret.

There are still some huge fish to be had, but they are not pushovers. Patience and persistence are virtues if a fly fisher wants to hook a fish there. The massive insect population is a double-edged sword that makes these trout such a challenge to catch. There is simply too much food available. Casting tiny midges to these trout is similar to false casting mosquito patterns for flying bats and swallows.

"There are some very large fish in those ponds," said biologist Hadley. "I'd say the average size is about 2.5 pounds, but there are some that reach double-digit weights. Casual fishermen won't catch those trout and even good fishermen shouldn't be ashamed to get skunked. I'd say a couple of fish is a pretty good day."

A couple of fish a day would be monumental for me. My success at Hog Hole has been limited to a zero fish tally during my three visits. The place seems to hold a curse over me.

During an initial trip, my single air chamber float tube blew out mid-Hog Hole. Kicking like a madman, taking gulps of water over the back of my waders, I barely managed to get to shore.

I ventured back a year later with a friend, Kent. We planned to fish the Hog Hole at midnight of opening day. When we arrived, the main access road was closed. We tried hiking to Hog Hole, wearing neoprene waders with float tubes laced to our backs. Five miles later, drenched in sweat on a moonless night, we finally found the hole.

Just after we geared-up, the wind grew in ferocity, frothing the water into whitecaps. Inside my waders I believe frost was building. Then, our olfactories went on high alert. Our chosen spot to wait out the blow was a sucker graveyard. Hundreds of rotting suckers were strewn around shore—probably the work of sadistic raccoons or just part of that curse. Snowflakes began falling from the sky. Kent was least happy. If you are not a patient fly fisher, Hog Hole may not be the ticket.

"I suggest being persistent, especially in Pond 3," Hadley said. "I know guys who fish that pond successfully, but they tell me the catch rate is lower than on the Hog Hole. There is a lot of food in all the ponds and that is why we see such good growth rates. But, throwing flies to those fish is just like being fed a slice of bologna after eating a prime rib dinner!"

One person who has experienced success at the ponds is John Oswald who works at Fish-On Fly and Tackle in Butte. He insists that those trout can be caught.

"I think it is a fun place to fish and you have the chance to take some really large trout," Oswald said. "We used to say an eight- to 15-fish day was good on the ponds, but I think the average has dropped off some. Still it holds huge fish; the largest rainbow I took was eight pounds and I caught a brown that was just under that. The largest fish I've seen taken was a 12-pound rainbow."

Major hatches in all of the ponds, which are strictly catch-and-release, include *Callibaetis*, damselflies, caddis and midges. There are also huge numbers of scuds, leeches and snails.

The big brown trout in Pond 3 get particularly active when the damsels come off. Browns up to 15 pounds have been taken from the pond and you might catch a fish with similar dimensions chasing damsel nymphs into shallow water.

"When the damsels are moving, those fish move out of the

Brown trout can grow quite large in the Gold Creek Ponds as evidenced by the author's catch, shown here.
Trout to 20 inches are not uncommon and hogs over 25 inches are often seen.

Although this small brook trout was taken on nearby Rock Creek, Georgetown Lake offers some enormous brook trout.

deep water and slurp along the banks," Oswald said. "A lot of the time they work most actively in the evenings. I just cruise along in my float tube, watching for rises and working those banks."

Leech patterns also draw strikes on the ponds and a size 2 or 4 brown Mohair Leech is always a good choice.

"You can't believe the number and size of the leeches in here," Oswald warned. "It's amazing; they look like water snakes."

◆

*Dense aquatic insect populations allow
the rainbow trout of Georgetown Lake to grow quickly.
Catching 10 fish over 18 inches is common on Georgetown
when its major hatches, like the damselfly emergence, are in progress.*

Pond 3, in particular, is best fished from a float tube or canoe. The banks drop off steeply and it can be difficult to reach fish from shore. However, on the Hog Hole and other ponds, you may want to leave the float tube behind.

"One of the secrets to fishing those ponds is to stalk individual fish that you spot from shore," Oswald said. "A lot of guys get out in float tubes and fish blind. They just drag a Woolly Bugger around for half the day. I like to just look for fish, try to figure out what they are eating, and then throw something out in front of them."

Of course, sight-fishing can be ruined when the wind pops up late in the morning. The best conditions bring no wind and an overcast sky. Bright days, in Oswald's opinion, are a "waste of time." Those big trout will bury their snouts in the weeds and you won't see any action until the sun goes down.

If you choose to fish the Hog Hole or one of the other ponds, from Missoula take the Warm Springs exit and turn left under the interstate. Follow the road for 100 yards and turn right. Follow that dirt access road to its finality. Then ford the Mill-Willow bypass to the ponds. Check the regulations thoroughly before you fish the area.

If you visit the ponds, arrive armed with a sturdy fly rod, plenty of patience and pray that a curse doesn't affect your success. And whatever you do, don't lie in a pile of rotting suckers. Three years after that rotting sucker debacle my waders still smell!

Upper River: Deer Lodge to Rock Creek

The afternoon PMD hatch was dead, the sun was dropping fast and caddis rose from the bankside brush, swarming over the water in droves—prime time! But where were those trout?

Below the mouth of Rock Creek, the Clark Fork's water quality rebounds. Here, the author, Moose and Shadow team up on a large brown that was hooked in deep water next to the rock bank.

I'd just floated several miles of the Clark Fork, from Garrison Junction downstream to the I-90 rest stop and I hadn't drawn a strike, although in one blind moment, I yanked a hopper right out of a huge brown trout's mouth. That fish measured over 20 inches long. I was devastated.

I swished down the last of a cracker with the tail end of my fourth beer (hey, it was hot, the trout weren't taking and that cracker was lodged painfully in my throat). Then I grabbed the oars and told my friend, Dan, to take a seat in the bow and return the contents to the cooler.

Few would feign surprise while listening to stories about tough fishing on this section of the Clark Fork; it suffers from chronic dewatering and high water temperatures during summer. Its trout population is paltry compared to sections of the river up and downstream. But, if you catch this section just after high water ends and before irrigators try to suck the river dry, you can nail some hefty browns. That's exactly why Dan and I were drifting down the river in my raft that mid-July evening.

According to Montana Department of Fish, Wildlife and Parks, brown trout populations from Deer Lodge to Drummond rate about 500 a mile. Best populations exist below the mouth of the Little Blackfoot extending to Drummond.

From Drummond to the mouth of Rock Creek, where dewatering is most acute, the population drops to about 30 fish a mile. Due to those numbers, few people fish that stretch of river.

It is unfortunate that populations rate so low below Drummond; that stretch carves between timbered slopes to the west and dry, sparsely timbered hills to the east. Often, the Clark Fork banks up against sheer, towering rock walls. The cliffs offer differing colors under varying light; purple, yellow, orange, blue—it is beautiful country.

It is also understandable why fly fishers avoid that water; even the best fly fishers with every trick in the book can't catch a fish some days.

Just like it does upstream near its headwaters, the Deer Lodge to Rock Creek section of the Clark Fork fishes best with caddisfly imitations most of the year. However, *Baetis* mayflies during spring and fall, pale morning duns in July and August, grasshoppers in July, August and September, and a few green and brown drakes during June and July also offer excellent opportunities.

When floating the upper river below Deer Lodge, do not expect to catch great numbers of trout. A big brown, like this fish caught near Phosphate, makes a slow day well worth it.

During April and May on the Clark Fork, March brown drake mayflies put rainbow and brown trout on the feed. Rating about a size 14 or 16, Sparkle Duns, cripples and even a standard Parachute Adams all imitate this insect nicely.

◆

As indicated, late spring, before runoff, and early summer, just after runoff, provide the best chance for success. But, fall is a good time to probe the river, too. Just make sure you focus attention at the mouths of feeder streams, like Flint Creek and Gold Creek.

Beginning in late September, extending through mid-November, the river's brown trout move to the mouths of those creeks and "stage" before sprinting upstream to deposit their eggs.

Big streamer fly patterns, like the Gray Ghost, Woolly Bugger, Zonker, or a sculpin will draw strikes. Because the holes below the tributaries can be quite deep, you may want to carry a sink-tip line along with a floating line. Run those patterns deep, strip them fast, let them swing through the tailouts—some meaty browns are sure to pound them.

Gold and Flint creeks offer excellent opportunities, too. However, private land borders much of their banks. Pound on a few doors, ask politely for permission and cross your fingers. If you do get on one of the creeks, throw large streamers in likely looking water; then hold on tight when you hook a big fish in such small water.

There are also a couple of notable stillwater options in the area. Just seven miles off the interstate, the Gold Creek dredge cut ponds offer some nice brown trout and a few stocked rainbows.

Watch for a nice *Callibaetis* emergence during spring and early summer. Midges may also be present. During late summer, hoppers can draw strikes. Always, a few caddis will be seen near the water. However, the best way to catch the ponds' trout is to throw leeches and Buggers up against the banks, which drop off drastically. A full-sink line is advantageous—the ponds are 30 feet deep in some places and that's where some monster browns, like an 18-pounder that succumbed a few years ago, hide.

In the Flint Creek drainage, Georgetown Lake offers one of the best options for large brook trout in the West.

The lake, which is nestled in a mountain valley at 6,000 feet, 20 miles west of Anaconda, also kicks out plenty of hefty rainbows. Brookies and rainbows to four or five pounds are not uncommon. Any place open to the public, where you can find brook trout of that size should rate high on every fly fisher's hit list. Somehow, Georgetown and its brookies do not get the credit they deserve.

In fact, the brook trout is universally unpopular in the West. Despite its colors, it is often regarded as an easier fish to take than rainbows, cutthroats or browns, and its fight is typically less pronounced when compared to the aerial antics of its cousins, particularly rainbows. Presented with the option to fish for any type of trout, brook trout would likely fall to the bottom of a Western angler's list.

◆

Bighorn sheep call the steep slopes above the Clark Fork home. While you could sight a bighorn from a raft on the Clark Fork in many places, they are most often seen near Rock Creek and again at Bonner. This willing model was seen in a field next to Rock Creek.

A large Alberton Gorge rainbow ready for release.

Below St. Regis, bighorn sheep are often spotted on the surrounding mountains. Sometimes they can be seen right off the road.

◆

However, a brook trout, with its olive, worm-tracked back, its white tipped fins and its orange-slashed sides, is a beautiful fish and many of them are not pushovers in Georgetown. In my mind, a colorful trout that weighs in from two to five pounds and offers a serious fly fishing challenge is a fish worth pursuing. And, Georgetown is the best water in western Montana to do just that.

Georgetown's big brook trout get most active in the fall when a friend of mine, who would rather not be mentioned, says, "there's a pretty good egg-sucking leech hatch."

To tempt the trout, throw large streamers, like Egg Sucking Leeches, Woolly Buggers, Zonkers and Mohair Leeches. And the

◆

Wildlife abounds along the Clark Fork.
During any float, you might see black bears, whitetail and
mule deer, bighorn sheep, numerous birds and maybe even elk, shown here.

fish are easy to find, especially along the east shore where natural springs are located. The brook trout will be nestled along the shallow-water gravel beds, guarding their nest and eggs.

While there are ethics to deal with when fishing trout on their spawning beds, the fishery remains open from the third Saturday in May through March 31. And, during fall those brookies are more than a little eager to smack a streamer.

If you do fish brookies during fall please do not take any home for the wall—take a photo instead. In my mind, fly fishers with lots of photos of big fish on their wall are cool. People who harbor a house full of fake-looking stuffed trout are reaching for something they will never find.

From opening day, the third Saturday in May, extending into September, Georgetown offers a variety of hatches and plenty of big trout, including three strains of fast-growing rainbows. But, it hasn't always been that way.

During the 1940s and 50s, before the national outdoor media discovered its tasty attributes, Georgetown Lake was one of the best trophy trout waters in the West. Large rainbows were numerous, five-pounders not uncommon. Then the lake was rocked by two major predators: anglers and the kokanee salmon. Fortunately, both play a lesser role in the fishery today.

Two major changes contributed to the rejuvenation of Georgetown's rainbow fishery. In 1985 the catch limit was changed from 20 brook trout and 10 other trout to a combined five trout a day. Also, FWP altered from stocking only Arlee strain rainbows to stocking Kamloops and Eagle River rainbows, too. The Kamloops and Eagle River fish are more predatory than Arlee 'bows and biologists hoped that those fish would put a dent in the kokanee population.

"As soon as we changed the regulations and the type of trout we were planting, we saw the maximum size and average size go up," biologist Hadley said. "We try to manage for a 14-inch average because almost nobody will scoff at a 14-inch trout. Some years we've been close to that average size, but we've never exceeded it. But, you have to remember, if that is the average size, there is a major fraction of larger trout in the lake."

Currently, the average rainbow goes 13 inches while the average brook trout goes 14.8 inches, which is up from 12 inches in 1990.

Prime hatches bring the best fishing opportunities at Georgetown, beginning with the *Callibaetis* mayfly emergence in May and June.

Expect excellent *Callibaetis* emergences during morning when the wind is calm and the fish are active. Big rainbows will cruise just under the surface sucking down emerging insects. Patterns with trailing shucks, like a size 12 Olive Sparkle Dun, do wonders during the hatch.

Georgetown's biggest hatch takes place around the Fourth of July when squadrons of damselfly nymphs let loose of aquatic vegetation and swim to shore. Fly fishers can work any depth of water with many different patterns (a size six or eight Six Pack works well). When the fish are on they'll drill those patterns. Using anything lighter than 5X tippet spawns frustration because a big fish may dive into the weed beds and break you off.

In late July and well into August, Georgetown offers an amazing caddisfly, a size 6 or 8 insect, for fly casters to mimic. According to Hadley, this is not a hatch for the faint of heart.

"These are great big caddis," he explained. "They are bigger than a golden stonefly and almost as big as a salmonfly. And the fish are looking for it. It comes off late in the evenings ... sometimes you can't see your fly, but you will know when you get a hit. It brings up the biggest fish so use

Spruce grouse can be found in the higher hills above the Clark Fork River.

heavier tippets or they'll bury themselves in the weeds and break off."

These caddis, which belong to the Limnephilid family, are rare on Western waters, as is their traveling preference. The big bugs swim to the shore instead of flying. Trout key-in on a wake that the insect leaves behind. Fly fishers should try to mimic that surface disturbance. Tom Thumbs, a large Elk Hair Caddis, Stimulators and even a clipped-hair body caddis on a size 8, long-shank hook work fine.

Interlude: Little Blackfoot

Just downstream from Deer Lodge at Garrison Junction, the Clark Fork receives a needed infusion of water from the Little Blackfoot River.

A colorful brown in the net.

While rafts and boats provide the best access to the Clark Fork, wading is productive, too. Author looks for Baetis-*scarfing risers as a raft passes by on the far bank.*

The Little Blackfoot, which flows into the upper Clark Fork near Deer Lodge, offers excellent opportunities for modest brown trout during the spring, summer and winter seasons.

It would be easy to cordially thank the Little B for its contribution and move downstream. But, the smaller tributary offers excellent fly fishing options.

Less recognized than its big brother, the Blackfoot, the Little Blackfoot fishes quite well during all seasons and some of its brown trout run to impressive size—16- to 20-inchers are not rare.

The successful fly fisher must seek productive water on the Little Blackfoot—some sections have been sabotaged by ranchers. Those sections hold skimpy trout populations and poor habitat. Other sections, however, will be noted as some of the finest looking small water habitat in the state.

Fly fishers should carry a variety of patterns when fishing the Little Blackfoot, its hatches can be diverse and heavy at times.

Beginning in the spring, before runoff, anglers will find the typical fare—blue-wing olives and some midges. For the olives, try the Olive Sparkle Dun, Parachute Adams, Olive Cripple or,

Not exactly showing off the best casting technique, the author works a heavily weighted streamer to a current seam.

of course, a Hare's Ear or Pheasant Tail Nymph prior to and during the infancy of the hatch. Watch for bugs on the water between 11 a.m. and 4 p.m. with peak activity between noon and 3 p.m.

In late spring (late April and May) look for the first solid caddis hatches of the season. The standard patterns, like Elk Hair Caddis, X-caddis, and Goddard Caddis work fine. Emergers like the LaFontaine Sparkle Emerger are productive, too.

Sometime in May, the river will blow out, turn the color of chocolate milk and send fly fishers away like it carried the plague. But, by mid-June or early July during excessive high water years, the river will drop into shape and provide some nice mayfly hatches. Watch for pale morning duns during late morning and midday hours. Try Sparkle Duns, Parachute PMDs and cripples.

As the PMDs subside, watch for a caddis flurry. Throw Elk Hair Caddis' and Sparkle Emergers late in the day and into dark.

Grasshoppers take plenty of fish during late summer and early fall and the standard variety, like Joe's and Dave's Hoppers work fine.

As the hoppers subside after the first few solid frosts of the year, watch for brown trout, both resident fish and monsters that move out of the upper Clark Fork to go on the spawn. They'll turn aggressive toward most streamer patterns; I've had the best luck with a size 4 brown Woolly Bugger, with long palmered brown hackle and a brown marabou tail. In the tail, I'll tie a few strands of olive sparkle.

Rock Creek to Milltown

The Clark Fork between the mouth of Rock Creek and Milltown Dam is possibly the river's most diverse section and I have held it in high regard since the first time I fished it; a modest brown rose up from a rock bank and pounded my Yuk Bug on the third cast of the day. Now that is the way to start!

The Clark Fork immediately becomes a better trout stream just below the mouth of Rock Creek where its flows are generous, insect diversity grows and the population of rainbows rises markedly. It is all good water.

Extending to Milltown Dam, fly fishers find an equal mix of browns and rainbows along with some of the best looking trout water on earth. There are narrow braids, long, deep backwaters, cut banks, rocky rip-rap banks, downed logs, and very deep holes. Unfortunately, trout that live there can be extremely picky, deciding to bite or not based on a set of factors unbeknownst to me. Is it the barometer? An influx of toxins rushing downstream from Anaconda? Could it be slight variations in flows? Or is it just the fish gods being finicky?

I don't know the answer and, to my knowledge, neither does anyone else. Due to that fact, it is always advantageous to call Doug Persico at Rock Creek Fisherman's Mercantile or one of the Missoula fly shops. Just ask this question: Is the upper Clark Fork fishing? If it is, insects are usually the reason why. When a hatch comes off, these fish will feed. And in that section, prime hatches begin in March and April when the *Skwala* stonefly emerges.

Less noted than the Bitterroot River's *Skwala* hatch, the Clark Fork's can be equally enticing—the fish are feeding on large stoneflies, there are very few people on the water, and, generally, the fish caught run large. Rubber-leg Brown Stones, Kaufmann's Stones, Bullet-head *Skwala*s and olive Stimulators draw strikes.

Floating, no matter where the hatch is coming off (excluding the headwaters), is the ideal way to fish the Clark Fork during spring and early summer. Rock Creek to Schwartz Creek Bridge and Schwartz Creek to Turah are excellent floats in the Rock Creek to Milltown section. You do not need to be a master at the oars to float this stretch, but it does harbor some narrow slots and tricky turns. Those downed logs can wreak havoc, too. Just pay attention to the river and keep a sharp eye out when rounding every bend.

There are numerous places where you will want to beach a raft and wade-fish prime runs and riffles. There are also some killer side channels and backwaters that hold some extremely large fish. Keep a sharp eye out for the mouth of feeder creeks, they will hold trout during spring and fall.

Following the *Skwala* hatch, look for a good emergence of March brown drakes. Caddis will be just behind them.
Then, in May, usually by the fifteenth, this section, especially below Rock Creek, gets a decent salmonfly emergence. Pound the banks with big, weighted Bitch Creek Nymphs, Kaufmann's Stones, and Yuk Bugs.

By the end of May, runoff will rip between the river's banks full-bore. The water resembles chocolate milk and effective fishing is an afterthought. Any float during high water can be suicidal. Black bear or shed antler hunting in the valley or up on the side hills is a good option.

After runoff, as the water clears and the riffles become defined, golden stones, yellow Sallys, PMDs, a few green and brown drakes and plenty of caddis take over. The caddis hatch rates most important and it will remain that way through summer.

In August and early September, fish caddis larvae patterns in the morning and dry or emergent flies in the evening. During midday hours, pop a size 6 Joe's or Dave's Hopper along

Flowing into the Clark Fork just 25 miles east of Missoula, Rock Creek offers all the habitat a trout fisher could ever want, plus scenery galore. Torrey and Skip Cenis work a nice run during a mid-June golden stonefly emergence.

Beargrass can be seen in the high mountains above the Clark Fork River during summer.

own—offers migratory Clark Fork browns.

While the upper Clark Fork is not known as a trophy trout stream, the fly fisher who seeks specific types of water and hunts big browns will find them.

Scott Brown of Missoula, a former Montana Grizzly football player who grew up on the banks of the Clark Fork at Turah, routinely pulls 20-inch plus trout out of the river. One brown that he caught weighed about 12 pounds. He's landed more Clark Fork trout between four and eight pounds than anyone I know. The reason: He hunts the backwaters and side channels religiously; he's not afraid to fish during relatively high water, when big trout congregate anywhere they can find a fresh flow entering the river; he carries a box of heavy-duty black Woolly Buggers.

I remember a day in May when the main river was nearly blown out by high flows. Brown introduced me to one of his favorite side channels. He pointed at a medium-depth hole and motioned me forward. I crept up the bank, glanced into the hole and nearly feinted. Near the bottom, huddled in a tight mass, was a ball of trout, a mix of rainbows and browns, that seemed eager to please. One cast was all it took. A healthy brown trout pounded my nymph, proceeded to trash the hole, then rolled over on its side and relented. That fish was one of the first brown trout I ever landed and the first of many I would take from the Clark Fork's side channels that spring.

On a subsequent trip, during early summer with the water slightly off-color, I chucked a Woolhead Sculpin into the riffle and allowed it to drop to the bottom of that hole. When it stopped I set the hook on what I thought was a rock. Then, the rod pulsed and my fly line moved to the head of the hole. Promptly, it began moving downstream (rapidly!) and my hook slid out of the fish. Was it a huge brown? A musty sucker? I will never know, but I will return and try to hook another fish like it.

the banks. Some healthy browns and rainbows will take those big terrestrials any time they see them.

During fall, run large streamers through the deep, dark holes and runs. Don't pass up the inlets of feeder streams, especially the mouth of Rock Creek. In fact, during fall, the lower 10 miles of Rock Creek—which merits a River Journal of its

◆

Probably the best way to probe the lower Clark Fork is with a raft or drift boat.

At Petty Creek the Clark Fork is a wide, intimidating river. Fortunately, it's eager, and often large, rainbow trout are more than willing to pluck dry flies off the surface.

Lake Missoula and the Great Flood

The Clark Fork may currently seem like a large river, but it hardly resembles its character 18,000 years ago when it was actually one of the world's most impressive inland lakes.

In fact, when fishing the Clark Fork today, consider the past—if you planted your feet on the banks of the river below Petty Creek today, you would be casting a fly 2,000 feet under the old lake's surface.

Lake Missoula formed when a tentacle of the Cordilleran ice sheet snaked down the Idaho Panhandle to the east edge of Lake Pend Oreille. It grounded out against the north edge of the Bitterroot Mountains, forming a 2,000-foot ice dam.

Behind the dam, the Clark Fork backed up on itself creating a virtual inland sea that covered 3,000 square miles, including the Missoula, Bitterroot and Deer Lodge valleys (an area about half the size of Lake Michigan). The lake reached 2,000 feet in depth (500 cubic miles total of water). The mountains outside of Missoula still harbor vestiges of the lakes shoreline; occasionally, a shell is unearthed high in the mountains.

Then, on a day when it would not have been advantageous to fish from an Achilles, Avon or float tube, Lake Missoula's ice dam lifted off the old river channel, floated, and broke apart. A 2,000-foot wall of violent water, traveling at speeds of at least 45 miles an hour ripped through the narrow valleys of northern Idaho and spread out in eastern Washington, shredding everything in its path. Through the Clark Fork Valley, the water moved at a volume of 8 to 10 cubic miles an hour. That is about 10 times the combined stream flow of all the rivers in the world today. Scientists believe such floods may have occurred 40 or more times.

Milltown to St. Regis

Between Milltown Dam and Petty Creek, the Clark Fork makes its most distinguishing change—from a small to medium size, brushy-banked brown trout stream, suited for nymphs and streamer flies, to a river of broad riffles, long glides, rocky, cottonwood lined banks, dry flies and big rainbow trout. That is a change that most of us accept eagerly.

The river broadens out and is more conducive to rainbows due to two major influences—the entrance of the Blackfoot River just east of Milltown Dam and the Clark Fork's confluence with the Bitterroot River near Kelly Island just 10 miles downstream from Milltown.

During wet summers, western Montana's wildflowers are especially impressive and abundant.

Even at East Missoula, the Clark Fork can provide some outstanding action. However, during high-water years, sediment rushes out of Milltown Reservoir and kills trout throughout this section.

◆

Immediately below Milltown Dam, the Clark Fork offers a large pool that harbors some sizable brown and rainbow trout and a pile of assorted scrapfish, like hefty suckers.

Downstream from the dam, the river curls through East Missoula, into Hellgate Canyon and exits into the heart of Missoula where fly fishers access some pretty decent after-work options.

One of the more noted runs, is at the entrance of Rattlesnake Creek. Some large rainbows and bull trout congregate there during spring and some resident fish are available all summer long. Aside from the mouth of Rattlesnake Creek, a few diversion dams and some powerful riffles, the Clark Fork's city section is a long, broad glide, ideally suited to dry flies.

All of the town section is paralleled by the Kim Williams Trail, which provides easy access to the river. It also offers interesting sidelights to the fishing. During spring, summer and fall, mountain bikers, hikers, dog walkers, drunk transients, bikini-clad sun bathers and the Montana Grizzly football team can be found along the trail. Naturally, some of those attributes are more appealing than others.

The trail also offers easy access to Missoula's downtown nightlife. Fish the afternoon PMD hatch or hit the evening caddis flurry, then make your way across the Higgins Avenue Bridge, the Orange Street Bridge or the University Foot Bridge and take up residence at McKay's (steaks, burgers, salads), Zimmorinos (pizza), McKenzie River Pies (pizza), the Mustard Seed (Asian), the Press Box (sports bar) or The Depot (steaks, burgers) for dinner. Or, if you're ready to quench a thirst, hit

Stockman's, the Rhino, Charlie B's, the Missoula Club or the Iron Horse. You probably don't want to show up in your waders at any of these places, but shorts, a T-shirt and Teva sandals are standard attire.

At Kelly Island, a large public access area located off of Spurgin Road near the mouth of the Bitterroot, fly fishers may find brown trout mixed in with rainbows and a few cutthroats.

Greg Henry of Missoula landed a 28-inch brown trout from the Kelly Island area and trout between 18 and 21 inches are fairly common. So are sightings of huge whitetail deer. If you are a hunter, seeing the big racked bucks of Kelly Island might send your mind spinning toward fall. During fall, beginning in September, bowhunters are allowed to hunt the area.

From Kelly Island, extending 12 miles downstream, past Council Grove and Harpers Bridge, to the Irskin access near Huson, the numbers of brown trout increase. Their numbers are not huge, however the adamant brown trout fisher can take some large trout on streamers and, during late summer, hoppers plopped noisily along the cut banks.

From Huson downstream to Petty Creek, the Clark fork is a lazy river, characterized by mile-long glassy glides, highlighted by a few broad riffles. Floating through this stretch on a warm, lazy summer day is ultimately relaxing; row from one side of the river to the other as you like, cast PMDs, Hoppers, Tricos, Hare's Ear or Pheasant Tail Nymphs to the banks. Cover the midstream risers. Let the oars rest, twirl down the river for a half-mile, take in the scenery, beach the raft for lunch, then continue downstream. Easy fishing, easy rowing, easy life on the Clark Fork.

That gentle nature changes downstream from Petty Creek Bridge. Oh, fly fishers will still find some long, flat stretches, but the riffles become more frequent, more violent, turning downright dangerous for the inexperienced at Rest Stop Rapid—the first of a series of rapids that are contained in the Alberton Gorge and Cyr Canyon.

◆

The Blackfoot River, which flows into the Clark Fork at Milltown, doubles the Clark Fork's water and dramatically changes the face of the river. Unfortunately, a proposed mine at the head of the Blackfoot could enhance sediment and heavy metal toxins flowing into the lower Clark Fork.

If you are going to take a day away from the Clark Fork River, the Bitterroot River is a good place to visit.

◆

Rest Stop Rapid is where drowned dogs, deer, cows, and humans accumulate after high water or when a murder takes place in Missoula. If police can't find a body, there's a chance it will show up at Rest Stop where all of the river's flow is forced between a rock wall to the north and enormous boulders to the west. As the water exits that short gorge, it forms massive whirlpools where those bodies congregate. The rapid has a way of trying to claim bodies on its own. Only the best oarsmen should attempt the rapid during elevated flows. Even during summer or fall, the lazy oarsman can get into trouble.

In the Alberton Gorge, which is located about 30 miles west of Missoula, the river offers excellent rainbow numbers and plenty of thrills. Many of those fish push 20 inches, but few anglers take the offering. Here's why: fly fishers like to float a river but few like to swamp their raft. And that can happen in Alberton Gorge, which harbors waves with names like Cliffside, Tumbleweed and Boateater rapids. One wave is referred to, affectionately, as Fang. With a name like Fang, it's not hard to see why some people avoid that water!

No matter where you fish between Missoula and St. Regis, fly fishers must hunt down pockets of water where pods of fish hold. Like the upper river, there are sections of the lower river that offer lots of trout and there are areas where you couldn't buy a fish, other than a slimy scrapfish, if your life depended on it.

That means, when floating the river in a boat or raft—the best way to fish the lower river (virtually a necessity in some sections)—you will push through idle water until you find a pod of risers, possibly drifting nymphs or streamers as you row.

When you first encounter a pod of Clark Fork risers, your jaw may simply drop, your mouth falling agape. Sighting 25 fish in a ten-yard pool, right next to the bank, gulping flies off the surface with an audible "pop", is enough to give even the most experienced angler a serious case of the shakes. You will see the heads, dorsal fins and slashing tails of trout that stretch to 20 inches with some regularity. Get tippeted down and have those flies tied on well in advance!

While the lower Clark Fork offers excellent green and brown drake, caddis, hopper, Trico and *Baetis* action, in my mind it's the pale morning dun hatch that offers the river's best overall experience.

In fact, in late July and August, just before summer and fall engage in their annual tug-o-war, the river's rainbows, especially those, it seems, between Petty Creek and St. Regis, turn ravenous.

On a typical day, you wrap both hands around your late-morning mug of coffee, take one last swig of the steaming, bitter liquid, then push a boat into the river's gin-clear currents.

Quickly, you're across the Clark Fork, under the Petty Creek Bridge, within a stone's throw of jealous travelers on Interstate 90. Your buddy holds the boat 25 yards off the steep north bank, right under the golden cottonwoods and big, green pine trees—right where you need to be. A glut of trout, all rainbows ranging from 10 to 20 inches long, slurp diminutive *Baetis* off the water's glassy, swirling surface.

◆

Most of the lower Clark Fork's rainbow trout average 16 to 18 inches, but some true hogs can be taken. Greg Henry shows off a fat rainbow.

Native westslope cutthroat trout are a possibility on the Clark Fork, however, due to shoddy land practices, their numbers are dwindling throughout the West. If you catch one, like this lower Clark Fork cutt, which ate a Parachute Adams during a fall Baetis hatch, please release it.

You throw a short cast downstream from the boat, quartering toward shore, where a current seam offers a smorgasbord to the trout. PMDs pop from the river's surface. Rainbows are hanging on the inside edge of a riffle where the current slows, just like they do almost every glorious late summer day, especially when the Big Sky is overcast.

You mend the fly line, flipping slack loops upstream, and that yellow Sparkle Dun, a PMD emerger pattern, dead-drifts in the foam with a dozen naturals. The trout are keyed-in on the bugs. But will they take yours?

A big 'bow darts from the depths and inhales your Sparkle Dun, a size 16 dry-fly that measures no larger than your smallest fingernail. Unfortunately, you set the hook too late—the trout spits a fake fly from its mouth, just like we might discard a shot of house whiskey when there's a bottle of Maker's Mark on the shelf!

Your buddy, knowing that he could have hooked that fish urges, "throw it in there again!" And you do. The trout cooperate. A similar fish, possibly larger, jumps your fly and this time you're on it. The beautiful buck rainbow leaps into the air, like two dozen brothers and sisters of his will do this day. The boat, a good friend and a realized dream splash downstream into your fondest memories. This is the Clark Fork. This is Montana. This is fly fishing at its best.

This summer float on the lower Clark Fork, you realize, is what fly fishing is all about. This, you understand, is why you survived early spring, when the rivers ran muddy, and maybe crowded, and the trout were almost impossible to catch. This day, you concur, may well make up for all those hours on the river when trout refused to take a fly and your frustration grew like ragweed. This time in Montana, during the PMD emergence, you believe, may be the best time all year for fly fishing. Your buddy is not about to argue. Why should he? You're on the river casting for trout that feed like there's no tomorrow while others are whiling away their lives in the narrow, stagnant confines of an office. Their measuring stick is money; yours, the number of trout to net.

Floating the lower Clark Fork during the PMD hatch, which may begin at 10 a.m. and last through evening, is a time to attain for all those days when the trout seemed uncooperative. Drift the river, catch-and-release those rainbows and watch the summer season pass. Enjoy the hot sun. Soon, cottonwoods will burst into color, Canada geese and mallard ducks will wing south, bull elk will be heard bugling in the trees, wood smoke will hang heavy in the valleys.

Interlude: Lower Clark Fork Tributaries

While the lower Clark Fork between Missoula and St. Regis offers excellent big water opportunities, there are several tributary streams worth noting. They offer excellent side trips away from the Clark Fork and harbor many of the big river's large migratory rainbow spawners during spring, after the general season opener, which traditionally arrives the third Saturday in May. Here is a run down on what to expect:

Rattlesnake Creek

There is a common misconception about Rattlesnake Creek—most fly fishers believe the river is closed to fishing from Beeskove Creek in the Rattlesnake Wilderness, all the way downstream to the creek's confluence with the Clark Fork in Missoula.

Actually, Rattlesnake Creek is open from its mouth, which pours into the Clark Fork just east of the Red Lion Inn, upstream to the Missoula water supply dam, which is about six or seven miles of water. However, the creek is closed all year between the dam and Beeskove Creek, which is about nine miles of very attractive water.

Fishing can be quite good in the open sections above and below the dam. Look for seasonal runs of rainbows, cutthroats,

A small Clark Fork tributary, Rattlesnake Creek offers an excellent diversion for Missoula-area fly fishers.
Jim Nave gears up for rainbow, cutthroat and, possibly, bull trout, twelve miles deep in the Rattlesnake Wilderness.

and bull trout in the lower river.

Often, the river can be blown out by the opener, lessening a fly fisher's opportunity to hit some of the bigger rainbows that move out of the Clark Fork. But, even if you miss the spawning run, there are good options through summer. Rainbows and cutthroats will rise willingly to a variety of mayflies and caddis. Watch for March browns, blue-wing olives and pale morning duns. Caddis are also present and they will be eaten by the Rattlesnake's trout between late May and September.

The lower Rattlesnake offers mostly pocket-water fishing with very few truly deep holes. It is highly wadeable, rating just 15 yards wide in most places.

To reach the upper river, you need a good set of lungs or a mountain bike. In my mind, a mountain bike, with full cargo stowed in a backpack, is the way to go. Many times I've taken off on a whim and pedaled upstream to Beeskove Creek and Franklin Bridge where the open section of the upper river begins. On a June or July day, with the sun beaming down, there are not many prettier places to be.

Fish the river anywhere above Beeskove and you will find good water. You will also find plenty of hungry cutthroat trout and maybe a few bull trout in the deep pools. It's all catch-and-release so bring food with you if you're staying overnight. And remember, there are grizzly bears and a ton of black bears in the Rattlesnake Wilderness (one time my friend, Hank, whistled around a corner on his mountain bike and nearly dusted an immature griz). Store and dispose of food properly.

There are decent caddis and mayfly hatches on the upper river and the standard patterns, like the Elk Hair Caddis, Pale Morning Dun, Hare's Ear, Pheasant Tail Nymph and Caddis Pupa, will take fish.

Woolly Buggers and large Woolhead Sculpins will draw takes from aggressive cutthroats, too. They may also draw strikes from bull trout, which run up to eight or 10 pounds on occasion. A 2X or 3X leader will hold a large fish if played properly.

Nine Mile Creek

Nine Mile Creek, an important spawning stream with decent populations of resident trout, flows into the lower Clark Fork River just east of Alberton.

On its lower end, the creek is bordered by much private property while its upper end offers access via the Lolo National Forest.

Throughout, the creek offers good fly fishing and some meaty specimens, rainbows, cutthroats and a few bull trout, for such a small creek—in most places it's a medium cast wide, which makes it unapproachable to those who would prefer to float.

Early in the year during high water (after the opener on the third Saturday in May), try large weighted nymphs, like a Kaufmann's Stone or Rubber-leg Brown Stone. When the water subsides, watch for decent PMD and caddis hatches extending from June through August. During fall, *Baetis* and general attractors will take fish. Woolly Buggers and Muddler Minnows draw strikes, too.

Although rainbows are the standard trout on Nine Mile Creek, you could bump into a cutthroat, like this 16-incher that was caught-and-released by Lauranne Billus.

While Nine Mile Creek can be tremendously frustrating to those who have trouble securing access, it is worth the effort. If all else fails, grab a bite to eat at the Nine Mile House, which serves excellent dinners and can have some entertaining nightlife on Friday and Saturday nights.

To reach Nine Mile Creek, take Exit 82 off of Interstate 90. Follow Nine Mile Road upstream.

Fish Creek

Fish Creek, one of the lower Clark Fork's most important spawning tributaries, offers excellent fly fishing for some nice rainbows and cutthroats and scenery galore. Just don't try to sneak on this creek before the opener (third Saturday in May). As they should, Montana Fish, Wildlife and Parks patrols the creek hard and they are eager to hand out citations. Fortunately, local judges don't look kindly on Fish Creek poachers—if they threw away the keys and closed the shades it wouldn't bother me.

One option is to fish the Clark Fork in Alberton Gorge just below the mouth of the creek; big rainbows, heading upstream to spawn will suck in streamers and large nymphs.

The upper portion of Fish Creek is accessible via the Fish Creek logging road. That section provides good fishing for smallish rainbows and cutthroats in the six- to 12-inch range, however some larger spawning rainbows can be encountered shortly after the season opens.

37

Fly selection can be crucial on the lower Clark Fork's flat-surfaced water. Jennifer and T.R. McCrystal search for the perfect PMD imitation. Excellent choices include cripples, extended body PMDs, Sparkle Duns and no-hackles.

The lower river can be accessed by hiking away from Fish Creek Road into a narrow canyon. Fly fishers encounter bouncy pocket water with some deeper pools. If you arrive early in the season, before high water or just after high water diminishes, you should find some large rainbows at the tailouts of the pools.

Throughout the creek, wading is the way to go. Floating is not an option.

Attractor dry flies work best on Fish Creek; anglers need a fly that floats high and is buoyant. Royal Wulffs, Stimulators, Elk Hair Caddis', Humpies and Renegades draw strikes. For the early season, don't be afraid to pitch larger nymphs and streamers, like Rubber-leg Brown Stonefly Nymphs, Woolly Buggers and Woolhead Sculpins.

To reach Fish Creek, take Exit 66 off of Interstate 90 just west of Cyr. Head south on Fish Creek Road. Private ranches border the river in some stretches, but the Lolo National Forest offers plenty of access and camping sites all along the road.

Most of the lower Clark Fork's fish are rainbows, but below St. Regis, fly fishers start bumping into more brown trout. While this 15-incher is average size, bigger browns, to 25 inches or more, are a possibility.

St. Regis to Lake Pend Oreille

The last quality trout water on the Clark Fork begins at St. Regis where the river breaks away from the drone of Interstate 90 and takes an astute north bend. Fly fishers refer to the area as "the cutoff."

Interestingly, the cutoff area, which extends from St. Regis downstream to Paradise and the confluence of the Flathead River, contains quality trout populations with some monster rainbows thrown in on the side. Despite that offering, it receives somewhat less pressure than the upper river. The chief factor for this light pressure is its distance from a city. It rests two hours driving time from Missoula and about three hours from Spokane, Washington. With such great waters, like the upper Clark Fork, the Bitterroot River, Blackfoot River and Rock Creek so close, that is a long way to drive for Missoulians. For Spokane residents, reaching the Clark Fork requires traversing two mountain passes, an out-of-state license and postponing a trip to the St. Joe or North Fork Clearwater. Regardless of distance traveled to reach it, those who fish the cutoff will find many willing rainbows and an awfully broad river.

What they will not find is huge numbers of trout. Whether floating or wade fishing the river (floating is the best way to go), fly fishers will locate various pods of trout with few found between. That means the prospective angler should push their oars through the slow sections. When a pod is located, drop anchor and thoroughly work the water.

While the average lower Clark Fork rainbow runs between 13 and 17 inches, there are some monster fish to be found near the cutoff. Two unverified reports of 30-inch-plus rainbows have surfaced in the last two years. Stories of huge trout, never seen and broken off, abound. One note for trophy trout seekers:

the St. Regis River is closed during the spring rainbow spawning run, but it remains open during the fall brown trout spawn; some huge browns can be found behind the large mid-stream boulders in the lower section of the St. Regis from late September through mid-November.

One reason why more large trout are not taken on the lower river is the method in which most fly fishers work that boiling water. Typically, dainty dry flies are thrown to risers. That tactic is not going to draw strikes from the largest trout. Instead, the patient angler, who can endure long bouts without a strike, would more likely suffer attack by using huge, six-inch streamers, tarpon flies and Lead-head Sculpins thrown off a full-sink line. Some of the lower river's holes are incredibly deep—in my mind a 20-pound brown or rainbow could easily show up.

The Flathead River flows into the Clark Fork at Paradise, increasing the river's volume considerably. Riffles become few, long, glassy, river-wide-deep runs and enormous, downright scary whirlpools persist. That water is best worked from a power boat.

Few trout call the last stretch of the lower Clark Fork home, but there are good numbers of smallmouth bass and northern pike between Paradise and Thompson Falls. In some places, backwaters that are accessible from the highway offer action on northerns.

Streamers are typical fare for both species. The smallmouths nail black and brown Woolly Buggers, Zonkers, Muddler Minnows, above and below the surface, and white Bunny Fur Leeches.

Clark Fork River Flies

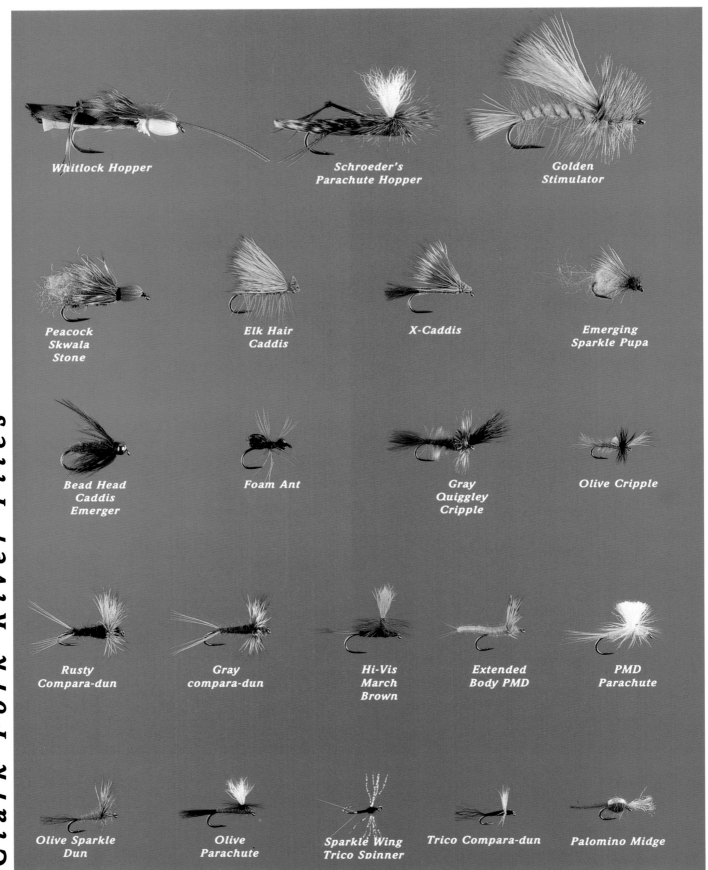

Whitlock Hopper

Schroeder's Parachute Hopper

Golden Stimulator

Peacock Skwala Stone

Elk Hair Caddis

X-Caddis

Emerging Sparkle Pupa

Bead Head Caddis Emerger

Foam Ant

Gray Quiggley Cripple

Olive Cripple

Rusty Compara-dun

Gray compara-dun

Hi-Vis March Brown

Extended Body PMD

PMD Parachute

Olive Sparkle Dun

Olive Parachute

Sparkle Wing Trico Spinner

Trico Compara-dun

Palomino Midge

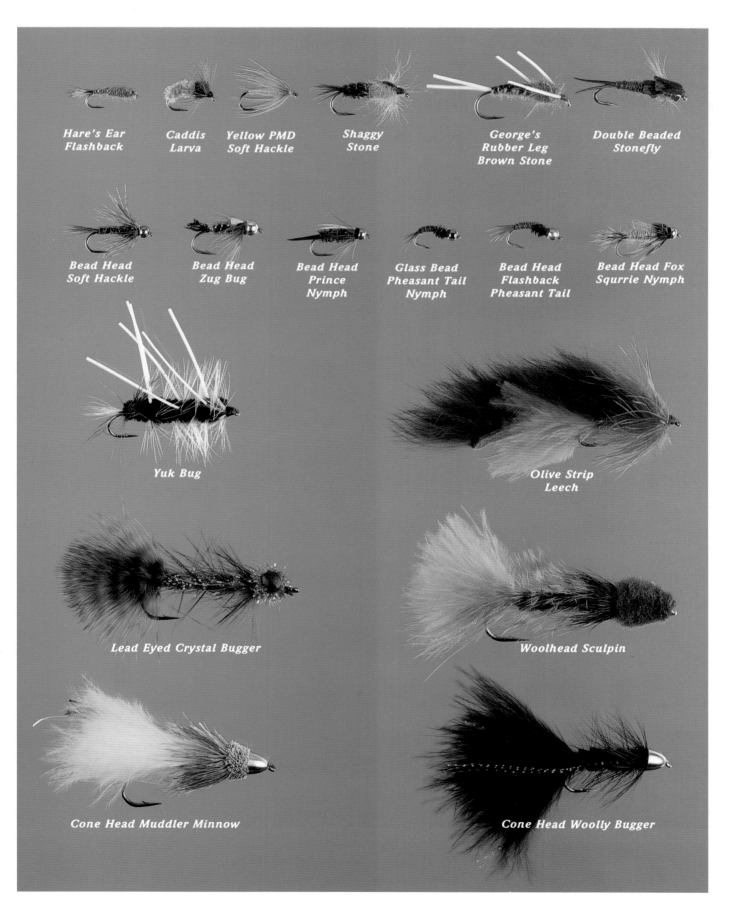

Hare's Ear Flashback

Caddis Larva

Yellow PMD Soft Hackle

Shaggy Stone

George's Rubber Leg Brown Stone

Double Beaded Stonefly

Bead Head Soft Hackle

Bead Head Zug Bug

Bead Head Prince Nymph

Glass Bead Pheasant Tail Nymph

Bead Head Flashback Pheasant Tail

Bead Head Fox Squrrie Nymph

Yuk Bug

Olive Strip Leech

Lead Eyed Crystal Bugger

Woolhead Sculpin

Cone Head Muddler Minnow

Cone Head Woolly Bugger

While the Clark Fork currently fishes "good", storms are brewing. Mining and timber harvest continue to plague the river and there seems to be no end in sight. Watchdog groups must protect the river.

The pike are suckers for five- to seven-inch-long yellow Bunny Leeches accompanied by 20-pound tippet. Pike are most active during spring and fall when they are in the weedy back-waters seeking small baitfish, birds, muskrats and mice.

You never know what streamer pattern will work best on the Clark Fork. Brian Murphy ties up a Yellow Yummie while Dan Summerfield entertains Shadow.

Interlude: Thompson River

The Thompson River flows into the lower Clark Fork just west of Thompson Falls and provides a tasty treat for those fly fishers who desire a day away from the big water.

The Thompson is a fun river to fish, due to its intimate size and its eager trout. In most places it is less than a double-haul wide.

The Thompson flows out of Lower Thompson Lake west of Kalispell and southeast of Libby. From there it cuts almost directly south 50 miles until it meets the Clark Fork. It offers easy access with two dirt roads paralleling the river for most of its length.

In its upper reaches, the Thompson twists through a series of pretty meadows before bolting down through a forested canyon, spreading out a little before it reaches the Clark Fork. Through those sections, fly fishers find a variety of water types and trout habitat. There are deep pools, slick glides, shallow riffles and boulder-laden pocket water. Four types of trout and one specie of char stalk the river.

Brook, rainbow, brown and cutthroat trout make up the majority of the catch, but a few bull trout strike up from the Clark Fork providing an element of surprise that only the unexpected big fish brings.

Most of the river's trout run eight to 12 inches, but there are some legitimate 20-inch rainbows to be had. Many of the larger fish are located on the lower end, likely spending part of the year basking in the big flows of the Clark Fork. These big fish represent the potential of the Thompson. With proper management and a helping hand from the river's anglers, large resident fish could be the norm on all reaches of the river.

In its upper ten miles, which run from the Murr Bridge upstream to Lower Thompson Lake, an angler will find mostly small cutts and brookies in the Thompson.

What those fish lack in size they make up for in eagerness to strike a dry-fly. And, because the Thompson runs particularly clear almost all year, even during spring run-off, it is a good bet when other rivers are blown out.

The river's prime hatches begin in May with a solid emergence of Grannom caddis and the early salmonfly hatch, which can draw those bigger fish to the top for massive dry-fly patterns. Because of the presence of salmonflies, a black or brown Kaufmann's Stonefly and Woolly Buggers work any day of the year.

Through summer a variety of caddis emerge; an angler should inspect these insects closely and choose the best match from their fly selection. Thompson River caddis may run the gamut in color, ranging from tan to olive to dark brown.

In August, grasshoppers, gray drakes and Trico and *Baetis* mayflies make their appearance. Gray drakes and *Baetis* should hatch best on overcast days, extending through September; the *Baetis* hatch into November.

Normally fly fishers are not required to match the hatch exactly. Oh, there are times when patterns and tippet make a difference, but normally the fish will rise steady to attractor patterns.

"Those fish are young and they act like it," offered Jim Vashro, regional fisheries manager for Montana Department of Fish, Wildlife and Parks. "Any of the attractor patterns will work. I like to use an Elk Hair Caddis or grasshoppers during late summer. Royal Wulffs and Renegades are good choices too, and they will work most of the year. Any of the nymph patterns, like a Hare's Ear or Prince Nymph will work and the streamers are good choices, too."

While fishing on the Thompson can be rated good, logging,

Shorebirds are common on the Clark Fork, especially around the ponds and sloughs at Warm Springs. Fall duck and goose hunting can be phenomenal in that area.

sediment overload and trout poachers weigh heavily on the river's potential. Its trout and char register numbers far less than what could be produced with prime conditions and considerate anglers. And it could use some special regulations placed on it. It had a seven-mile section reserved for catch-and-release angling, but that provision was dropped by FWP in 1990. Most of the Thompson's anglers called that section "Closed," which should give a clear indication of their mentality. Meat-sackers is the correct term, I believe. FWP's decision to drop the catch-and-release section left the Thompson with little hope of becoming a significant trophy-trout fishery.

"There was a lot of non-compliance when we had the catch-and-release section," Vashro admitted. "Plus that section

This rainbow, caught-and-released by Kent Sullivan of Missoula, is a typical lower Clark Fork fish.

When caddisflies hatch on the Clark Fork, especially in the upper reaches above Deer Lodge, they emerge en masse. Hold your breath, tie on a LaFontaine Sparkle Pupa and prepare to slay.

was too short. We had fish moving 20 miles, right out of the catch-and-release area and into places where it is legal to catch them. In order to make the regulations work, we need to put them on a large section of the river, like 20 miles or even the whole thing, but we don't have public support for that type of management yet."

That does not mean the Thompson won't hold a population of big fish in the future. A curious phenomenon occurs when fisheries are stripped of their large trout. Often, fish-bonking phenoms turn pro-active. They blame everyone except themselves for the trout's demise, then quickly support restrictive regulations.

"I think this fishery will continue to slide downhill," Vashro said. "There are about 400 to 500 fishing days a year, per mile on it. The number of large fish in the river is way down compared to the past. At some point, the quality will drop to a level that is unacceptable. Then, people may support our efforts. Until that time, you won't see many large fish in the Thompson."

Conclusion: Take a look in the mirror

I can remember clearly a foggy September afternoon on the lower Clark Fork with a friend, John Huber, in my boat. I was pulling ours, allowing my guest to fish. I owed him that privilege. He put me on some huge browns the previous season in central Idaho.

I had seen Huber fish better than he did that day on the Clark Fork. He was shaking off a serious case of the bottle flu, brought on by a night of wildness in Missoula.

Despite his fuzzy head, weak stomach (during our drive to the river he said, "Hey, Thomas, can you pull this truck off the road in two seconds?") and less than perfect presentations, Huber fully appreciated the Clark Fork—a river that most outsiders hear few good things about.

Floating from Petty Creek downstream through Rest Stop Rapid, we encountered rising fish the entire way. Those rainbows and cutthroats were gulping *Baetis* mayflies like there was no tomorrow. Canada geese passed overhead. Whitetail deer bounded through the bank-side willows. Mule deer grazed on the high slopes above the river and bugling bull elk would make their presence known as soon as the sun set. The old Burlington Northern jealously blew its horn when passing; Huber was hooked up to another sweet rainbow.

That day typified the Clark Fork at its best; when the fish are on, whether it's brown trout eating caddisflies on the upper river or big rainbows slurping *Baetis* on the lower sections, you cannot beat it.

As the light faded and I made the last few pulls on the oars, having successfully negotiated Rest Stop Rapid which nearly ate two of our friends who proceeded us, Huber, who guides year-round on tremendously challenging Silver Creek, remarked, "It's nice to see that there are trout like this in a river like the Clark Fork. I never knew anything about it before I came here, but I could tell it was a good river the first time I saw it. The Clark Fork is a beautiful river and I can't believe that these rainbows can be so easy. This is really easy fishing. I like it."

The Clark Fork can be like that. It's a river that beckons for 250 miles as you follow its banks driving along Interstate 90 through western Montana. You'll see deep, alluring pools, perfect long riffles, deep undercut banks and, of course, rising fish.

Despite its offerings, some fly fisher's focus only on the Clark Fork's past—those days when the river ran red. What those skeptics fail to realize is this: the Clark Fork is not dead—far from it—and its attributes, though scattered, rank right up there with any of the big hitters, like the Big Hole and Beaverhead. By simply giving up on the river they are missing fantastic fly fishing opportunities for some awfully large trout. Maybe more importantly, they are turning their backs on one of the West's most important indicator rivers. You and I could do the same, but the fate of the Clark Fork and its tributaries represents the eventual fate of all Western trout waters. If we let the Clark Fork go, eventually we will find the number of quality trout streams far from acceptable and we may all cry the blues together—standing elbow to elbow, dodging backcasts and extricating barbed hooks from each other's ears on what water we have left.

The next time you visit Montana, your truck pointed toward some big-name stream, allow yourself a day on the Clark Fork. Consider the river's past and its muddled future—your favorite stream could be next. While you consider that sick notion, get your fly on the water, the Clark Fork's dry-fly smashing rainbows and Bugger-eating browns should not disappoint.

Planning Your Clark Fork Trip:
The merits of hiring a guide

The Clark Fork is big, intimidating water on its lower end and tricky, temperamental water on its upper reaches. To the visiting fly fisher, booking a guide can only help you gain confidence while fishing the river.

Standard guide rates in Montana fluctuate from $240 to $300. That price will provide one guide for two people, a drift boat or raft if you need one, a very hearty lunch (a guide should provide more food and drink than required), shuttle service, and plenty of great conversation. You can book guides through the Missoula fly shops (Grizzly Hackle, The Kingfisher or Missoulian Angler) or through Doug Persico at Rock Creek Fisherman's Mercantile.

Gear: Do not skimp

Rods

Resident and visiting fly fishers should not jeopardize a day on the Clark Fork with flimsy equipment. It is true, you can get by with a relatively inexpensive outfit, however, you certainly cannot count on an outfit like that to perform admirably in varied conditions. Those cheap noodle sticks are death when the wind comes up.

Large trout are available in the upper Clark Fork, below the Anaconda Settling Ponds, throughout the year. The author hoists a snakey 26-incher just before release.

If I had to pick one all-purpose rod for the Clark Fork, I would choose a 9-foot, 6-weight; it is heavy enough to punch through the wind, it has enough backbone to allow landing a large fish quickly, and yet it is light enough that you will still garner a fight from a 12-inch trout. There may be more ideal rods for certain situations, but you can get away with a 9-foot, 6-weight in any situation.

With that said, a 9-foot, 5-weight is not a bad rod choice either—ideal when the wind is down. And, a 9-foot, 4-weight is killer for the flat water stretches and feeder creeks, which may require long, light tippets and heavy-duty stealth.

Personally, I like Sage and Orvis rods; they are durable, reliable and handsome. I have used a 9-foot, 6-weight Sage, a high school graduation present from my family, on many waters in the West and it's never failed me; it's accounted for rainbows up to eight pounds (released) on the Blackfoot Reservation lakes, and a 42-inch buck steelhead (released) in Alaska. And, after an hour-long marathon, I actually landed a 46-pound king salmon (released) on it, again in Alaska.

The Orvis I fish is a 9-foot, 5-weight Trident. It has a fast action and plenty of power for a five-weight. It is an ideal rod for large rivers, like the Clark Fork.

Both Orvis and Sage back their rods with guarantees; snap it in a truck door or while fending off a rattlesnake or rouge skunk and they'll replace or fix it free of charge. That is an enormous bonus when using a rod that may cost a few hundred dollars.

Leaders

For a week-long stint along the Clark Fork, you will want to carry plenty of packaged, knotless leaders. And you will want to have a varied supply. Do not head out on the river for a day without at least two 6X, two 5X and two 4X leaders. The 6X is ideal when fishing small dry flies on flat-surfaced water to selective trout. In some situations, you cannot get a trout to rise on anything heavier than 6X.

A 5X tippet is the most versatile leader for Montana. It is light enough to fish dry flies, yet heavy enough to throw a weighted nymph. Plus, if you encounter some selective fish, you can tie a section of 6X tippet (from a spool) onto it.

Flies

I try to carry as many fly patterns as possible. Every year I read articles by various outdoor writers who claim the entire spectrum of aquatic insects can be covered with, say, 10 or 12 patterns. You've seen those articles, "The Dirty Dozen" or "The Top Ten."

I don't believe those words because each season I find myself rummaging through my fly boxes, loaded with dozens of patterns, unable to select the proper imitation.

The stocked fly box will harbor patterns to match various mayfly, caddis, stonefly, midge, moth, terrestrial and minnow species. And it will cover all stages of the hatches.

Whether you are fishing one of the Clark Fork's tributaries, like the Thompson, or the main river itself, be prepared for unusual weather—western Montana doles it out eagerly. Kent Sullivan endures a wicked hail and rain lashing during a memorable fall float.

Fall colors can be found all along the Clark Fork. These trees, located in the Dry Creek drainage, are particularly nice.

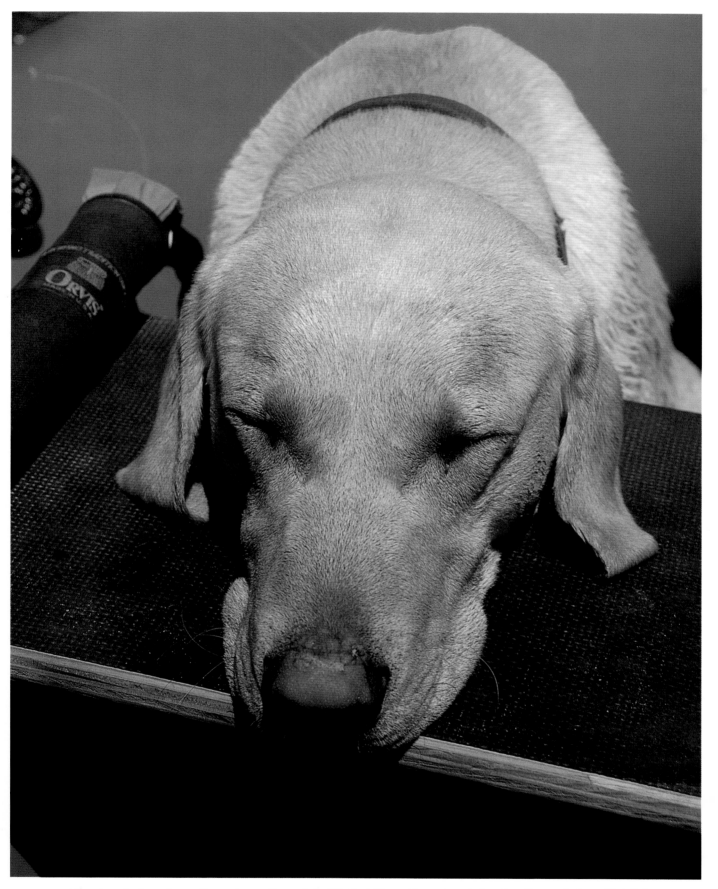

After a long day in a raft, even the most energetic can feel a little tired. Moose takes a siesta during a long float on the lower Clark Fork.

Not as common as rainbow or brown trout, a native cutthroat is a fish to be admired.
The author hooked this westslope cutt on a diminutive Baetis pattern in October.

Weather

Hey, you know the weather; no matter where in the world you are at any given moment, anything can happen.

In western Montana, we've seen six inches of snow on the ground in July. However, on a normal July day, the temperature will peak somewhere between 80 and 90 degrees. During spring, the temperature can range between 10 and 80 degrees. During winter—well, it's pretty darn cold on almost any given day. No matter what the weather rates, you will need a pair of waders unless you are wet wading on a sizzling summer day.

I have used various brands of neoprene waders and I find that Orvis and Simms are extremely durable and reliable. A 4mm or 5mm rating will keep you warm when the water is cold. I wore my pair of Orvis Battenkill Guide waders in the Gallatin River one December morning with the air temperature hovering at 5 degrees and ice building in the river from the bottom up! I remained warm for the three hours I spent in the river—and caught a couple browns over 17 inches! During summer, if I am not wet wading, I'll wear a pair of light, breathable waders.

Rain can also factor into a Clark Fork fishing trip. A Gore-Tex® coat, like an Orvis, Patagonia or Streamline will shed that water like a seal skin. Combined with neoprene waders, a Gore-Tex® coat provides an invincible shield against the wind and rain.

Flying in and getting around

You can fly into Missoula, Montana by commercial jet service, but your arrival is always weather dependent.

When you travel to Montana, try to keep all your essential gear in a carry-on bag—rods, reels, a vest, camera and flies should be packed with you. No need to tempt disaster by checking your baggage.

Although they are not commonly caught on the Clark Fork, bull trout are present. Justin Adams, son of former Phoenix Sun, Alvan Adams, prepares a nice bull trout for release.